FOR ALL THAT FEEL

Jeri Speaker

Copyright © 2012 by Jeri Speaker. 121297-SPEA
Library of Congress Control Number: 2012918771

ISBN: Softcover   978-1-4797-2915-9

All rights reserved. No part of this book may be reproduced or transmitted in any form or by any means, electronic or mechanical, including photocopying, recording, or by any information storage and retrieval system, without permission in writing from the copyright owner.

This is a work of fiction. Names, characters, places and incidents either are the product of the author's imagination or are used fictitiously, and any resemblance to any actual persons, living or dead, events, or locales is entirely coincidental.

To order additional copies of this book, contact:
Xlibris Corporation
1-888-795-4274
www.Xlibris.com
Orders@Xlibris.com

Would like to give a shout out to those who stuck by me throughout the years. A special thanks to those who were there for this, what I hold dear Melissa Deoram, Johnny Mays and Sima Culjak.

TO BE ALIVE

If at any point you feel strong
Store it where you can't forget
When trouble times arrive your way
Remember you are strong it's stored away
Don't give up looking you will find that strength
Believe in yourself you will conquer the day
Remember you are not the only one
We all have our share of pain & suffering
Remember what living is and what it's about
It is not what we have or want
It is all about how we live

Tomorrow will come

Your heart breaks
As life goes on
What is anything
If your body is gone
Keep up your spirits
For it is your strength
Your heart only a tool
God determines the length
Don't fret, no time to worry
Live today tomorrow will come
For life is short enough
We should learn to always have fun

SHATTERED DREAMS

There's people we hurt
People we shouldn't
People who you make cry
That you think or wouldn't
People we respect or don't
Others are just to love
After those to love you've hurt
Start praying to the one above
For dreams are shattered
Feelings torn all apart
Little minds hard to repair
Remain forgiving, but grow alert
Once trust is taken away
There's nothing really left
They're left with obligations
Only a life long debt

NAÏVE

Our hearts open
Easily to be bruised
Our minds closed
But easily confused
Left in this state
We are easily used
Taken advantage of
Set up for abuse
Close your heart
Open your mind
Life can be wonderful
It is yours to find
With your mind open
You may see the sign
So find a happy place
In your mind for it to stay
One no one can find
Where all evils stay away

My word is bond

My heart bleeds for you
I know how you really care
I don't know what I want
Or if I want anyone there
But if I chose to give it a go
And you've proved yourself to me
I will give you a promise then
You will be the only one I see

Blinded

Born innocently, strung along
Raised right or wrong
When grown, choices our own
Ignorance is bread
It is what's read
Open your eyes
See the lies
Enter each day
With thanks and pray
Open our minds
Seek you shall find
Perfection not for you or for me
But your eyes should be open just to see

As we test

How often can we test the waters
There must be a line to draw
How often do we stomp or be stomped
Before out comes the claw
We often push buttons right and wrong
Not for the good but to find flaw
No matter how the waters test
There is a line, a line to draw

Solid as a Rock

I admire you from afar
You have qualities hard to find
You are strong with heart
You're very patient and kind
You are what all people should be
An example people should see
These things you already know
And many more know it is true
Knowing you I feel blessed
You're a special person, Thank-you

Addiction

Something that takes you over
We're hooked before it's discovered
Our body is lingering around
Our mind not totally sound
Looking at ourselves from outside
Caring really nothing of pride
Our insides an empty shell
We fall deeper into the well
Feeling nothing time & time again
Just believing the bad will end
Help is around if we take time to see
We have the strength, we must believe
Patience a must as well as time
What ever was lost, "we can find"

The simple life

Day by day as life goes on
Think why we are here on earth
We all have purpose for our being
There's a reason for everyone's birth
Live life to the fullest, respectfully
If we ever have any doubt
There are always options, roads to turn
People aren't perfect, god will help us out
Pray for strength in our own weaknesses
Just to help make it through life
Pray for the art of understanding
For this will help us to strive

A Love So Strong

A love so strong
What went wrong
I thought it forever pure
Now lost, never to be sure
My heart left broken
My mind stirred and shaken
My body feeling drained
As my soul is strained
To give and give my all
Too still watch it crumble & fall
Please explain, what went wrong
A bond meant to be so strong

A LIFE SAVED

We don't always see eye to eye
There's even times we've both said good-bye
I am sure we always hurt each other
That happens when you're constantly together
Our very clashing differences, in spite of
We made it through just on our love
You were not always there for me
I sure didn't make it very easy
I am very grateful for the life you gave
Thanks for a life you don't even know you saved

Art of growing

The art of growing
Is learning not knowing
As honey is gold
We all grow old
Once upon a time, so naïve
Now believing what we believe
Gaining insights
Taking new flights
To take a chance
Is to have life enhanced

Life Without a Dream

Life without a dream I'm not sure how it would be
Maybe it would be like life without reality
A dream is not a fantasy it's something kind of neat
Nor is it a vision because dreams are always sweet
Life without a dream would give us no future to see
Would stop us hoping and becoming all we could be
A dream can be the greatest feeling inside
When they become reality you feel the pride
Life without a dream it doesn't seem worth living
It can't hurt the heart it's only your mind you're giving
So when a dream gets broken and you're feeling blue
Get your mind together and dream of something new

Just another day

What's happening I don't know
I try I give everything I have
Hurt I'm led astray, what's happening
My soul empty with nothing left to give away
This path by my soul is so unfamiliar
Not wanting to stroll that path again
To give all and receive nothing at all
It's not selfish but my heart can't win
Take time to breathe deeply, in & out
Forget your troubles, letting them go away
Know everything happens for a reason
Breathe, pray, just believe there will be another day

Hurt by love?
Haven't we all
Get over it baby!
It's a stumble, not a fall.

Friendship

Forever, always, until the end
Rushing to help, always a hand to lend
Is always by your side good or bad
Even gives you advice whether it makes you mad
Never knocking you down, your spirits they lift
Dependable, reliable a very precious gift
Selflessness, a kindness that is hard to find
Hands full of hope; a heart that's open wide
In time of need they make you feel good inside
Patient, forgiving, honest and true
So most of all I'm glad I found one in you

Missing you

Missing you
Doesn't make me blue
Remembering you
Helps me make it through
Thoughts of you
Bring smiles which help too
Just knowing you
Makes me feel alive and new
My love for you
Keeps me from really missing you
So thank you
For just being you

WORLD IN A WHOLE

Hustle, bustle and more hustle
The world in a whirlwind
How do we slow it down
Pace life out til' its end
Together life can be magical
Sharing the growing experiences
Learning others life styles
Dealing with lives differences
Perfection far from logical
Simplicity is what we should ask
To expect a perfect world
It is just too hard a task

What Matters

What really matters
Not what you can give
Not what you have
But the way you live
What really matters
Not the way we all are
Not the negative feelings
But a child's eyes lit like stars

THINK STRENGTH

Get up and go
Put on a show
Forget you're hurt
Just let it all go
Hold on tight
Put up a fight
Don't ever give in
Take a different flight
The man high above
Will provide the love
Look for the signs
Not as white as a dove
So get it together
No matter the weather
Enjoy your life
Every breath's a treasure

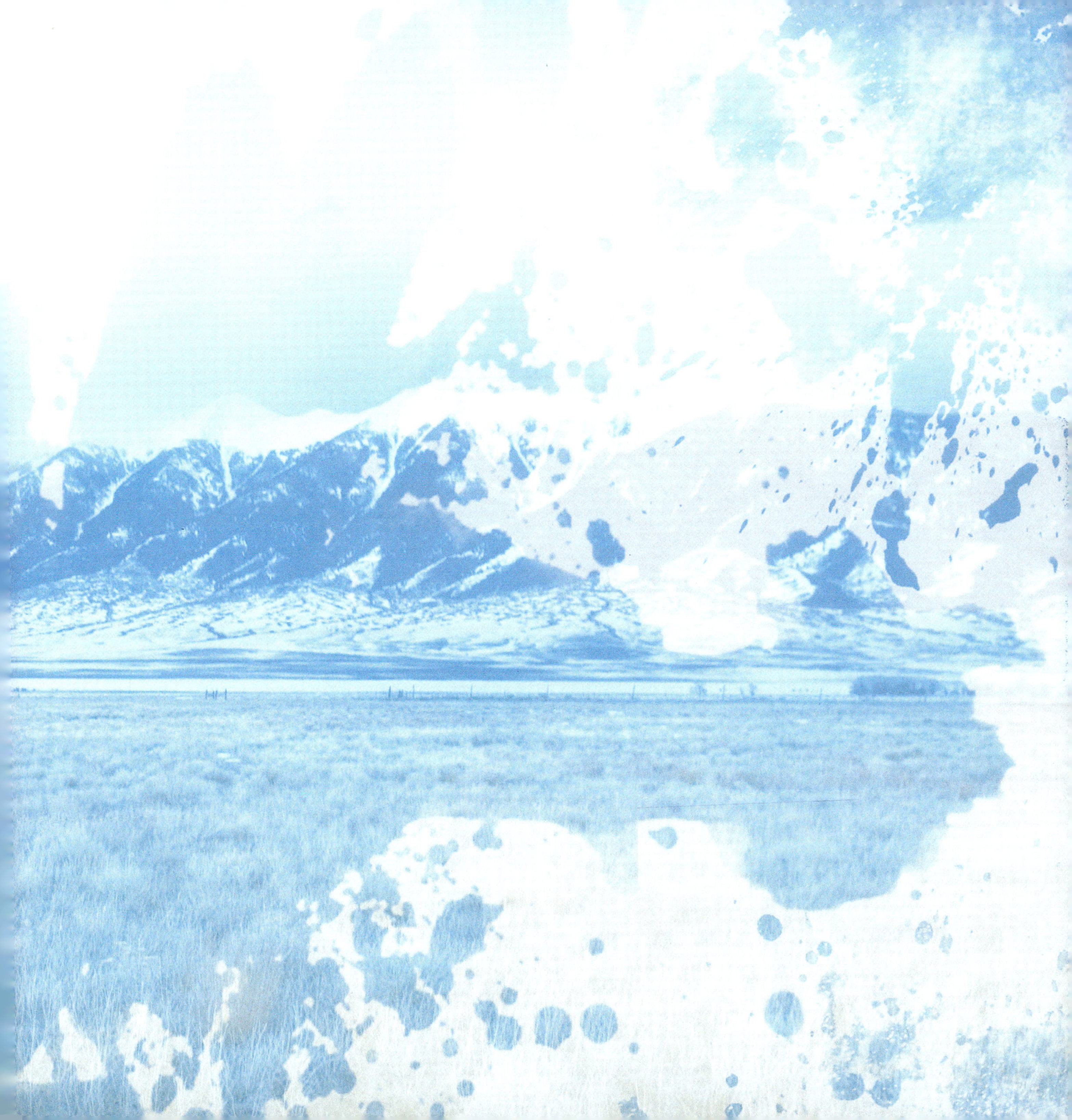

To Be Alive	January 31 2002
Tomorrow will come	October 1 1998
Shattered Dreams	late Summer 1997
Naïve	Winter 1997
My word is bond	Winter 1997
Blinded	July 1 1998
As we test	July 1 1998
Solid as a rock	July 29 1998
Addiction	May 21 2000
The simple life	June & July 1998
A love so strong	February 21 2003
A life saved	February 16 2002
Art of growing	April 16 2000
Life without a dream	Winter 1997/1998
Just another day	July 1 2000
Friendship	Winter 2001
Missing you	2000 copyright
World in a whole	
What matters	March 1 1998
Think strength	January 13 2005

Edwards Brothers Malloy
Thorofare, NJ USA
April 8, 2013